Rising Stars

ROBERT PATTINSON

By Maria Nelson

Gareth Stevens
Publishing

Please visit our website, www.garethstevens.com. For a free color catalog of all our high-quality books, call toll free 1-800-542-2595 or fax 1-877-542-2596.

Nelson, Maria.
 Robert Pattinson / Maria Nelson.
     p. cm.
 Includes bibliographical references and index.
 ISBN 978-1-4339-5900-4 (pbk.)
 ISBN 978-1-4339-5901-1 (6-pack)
 ISBN 978-1-4339-5898-4 (library binding)
 1. Pattinson, Robert, 1986—Juvenile literature. 2. Motion picture actors and actresses—Great Britain—Biography—Juvenile literature. 3. Singers—Great Britain—Biography—Juvenile literature. I. Title.
 PN2598.P36.N45 2011
 792.02'8092—dc22
 [B]

                                    2010046425

First Edition

Published in 2012 by
Gareth Stevens Publishing
111 East 14th Street, Suite 349
New York, NY 10003

Copyright © 2012 Gareth Stevens Publishing

Designer: Katelyn E. Reynolds
Editor: Kristen Rajczak

Photo credits: Cover, pp. 1–32 (background) Shutterstock.com; cover, p. 1 Shutterstock.com; p. 5 Ian Gavan/Getty Images; p. 7 Martin Bureau/AFP/Getty Images; p. 9 David Westing/Getty Images; pp. 11, 21 Dave Hogan/Getty Images; p. 13 Dave M. Benett/Getty Images; p. 15 Pascal Le Segretain/Getty Images; pp. 17, 19, 23 Kevin Winter/Getty Images; p. 25 Kevin Winter/TCA 2009/Getty Images for Fox; p. 27 Robyn Beck/AFP/Getty Images; p. 29 Jon Furniss/WireImage/Getty Images.

Printed in the United States of America

CPSIA compliance information: Batch #CS11GS: For further information contact Gareth Stevens, New York, New York at 1-800-542-2595.

Contents

Meet Robert

Robert Pattinson is an actor. Millions of people have seen his movies.

Across the Pond

Robert was born on May 13, 1986.

He is from London, England. Robert now lives in Los Angeles, California.

Robert started acting when he was in high school. He was in stage plays. Robert also worked as a model.

Movie Magic

Robert's first big movie came out in 2005. It was called *Harry Potter and the Goblet of Fire*. He played Cedric Diggory.

Katie Leung

Stanislav Ianevski

Clemence Poesy

Rupert Grint

Daniel Radcliffe

Emma Watson

11

Robert acted in two TV movies in 2006 and 2007. In 2008, he played Art in the movie *How to Be*.

A Star on the Rise

Robert starred in *Twilight* in 2008. It made him a star! Robert played a vampire named Edward Cullen.

Twilight made about $70 million its first weekend. It was in movie theaters for 19 weeks! Robert won a lot of fans.

twilight

Kristen Stewart

Robert played two songs on the *Twilight* soundtrack. He sings and plays guitar on the songs "Never Think" and "Let Me Sign." Robert knows how to play the piano, too.

Series Sequels

The second *Twilight* movie came out in 2009. It's called *New Moon*. The movie made more than $26 million at the first midnight showing alone!

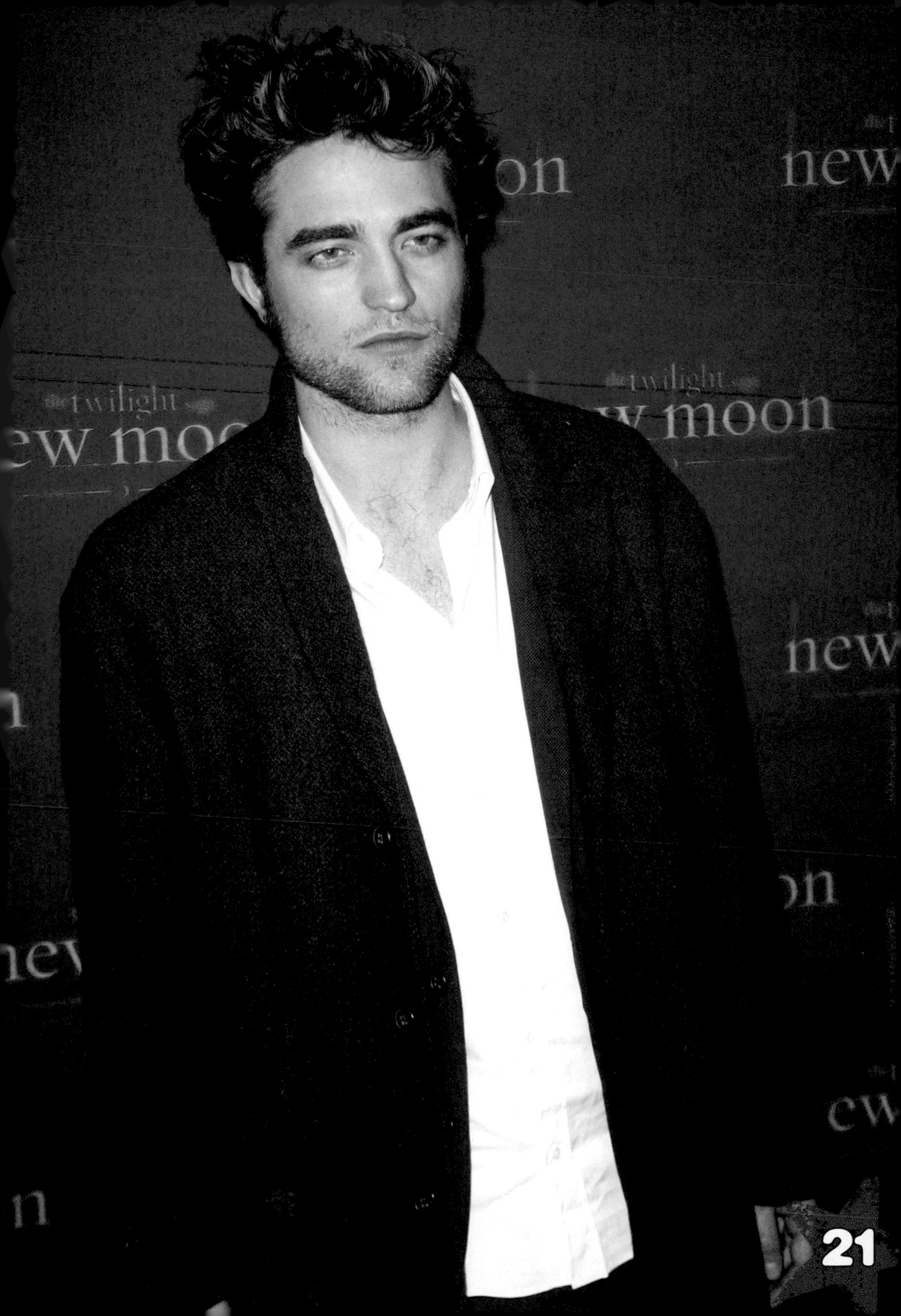
twilight
new moon

The Twilight Saga: Eclipse came out in 2010. Robert played Edward Cullen again. He is also in the final movies, *Breaking Dawn Part 1* and *Breaking Dawn Part 2*.

Taylor Lautner

Beyond Twilight

In 2010, Robert starred in another movie, too. It's called *Remember Me*.

He also won four Teen Choice Awards!

In 2011, Robert starred in *Water for Elephants*. Reese Witherspoon was in it, too. The movie is based on a book.

Robert has fans all over the world!

What do you like about him?

Timeline

1986 Robert Pattinson is born on May 13.

2005 *Harry Potter and the Goblet of Fire* comes out.

2008 Robert stars in *Twilight*.

2009 Robert stars in *New Moon*.

2010 Robert stars in *Eclipse*.

2011 *Water for Elephants* comes out. *Breaking Dawn Part 1* comes out.

2012 *Breaking Dawn Part 2* comes out.

Books

Besel, Jennifer. *Robert Pattinson.* Mankato, MN: Capstone Press, 2010.

Rusher, Josie. *Robert Pattinson: True Love Never Dies.* London, England: Orion, 2008.

Websites

Robert Pattinson

www.imdb.com/name/nm1500155/

Find out more about Robert Pattinson and his movies.

RobertPattinson.org

robertpattinson.org

Keep up with Robert Pattinson and *Twilight* news.

Glossary

award: a prize given for doing something well

model: a person whose job is to show clothes or other things for sale

soundtrack: the music used in a movie

stage: a raised area where plays are shown

theater: a building in which movies are shown

vampire: a made-up being who drinks human blood

Index